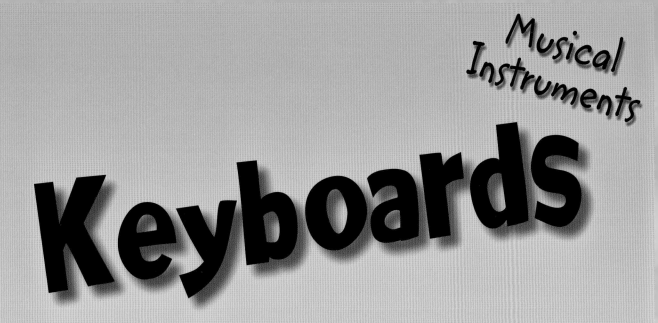

Musical Instruments

Keyboards

Wendy Lynch

Heinemann
LIBRARY

Customer Service 888-454-2279
Visit our website at www.heinemannraintree.com

Designed by Joanna Hinton-Malivoire and John Walker
Printed in China by South China Printing Company

10 09 08 07 06
10 9 8 7 6 5 4 3 2 1

New edition ISBN: 1-4034-8865-7 (hardcover)
                     1-4034-8871-1 (paperback)

The Library of Congress has cataloged the first edition as follows:
Lynch, Wendy, 1945-
       Keyboards / Wendy Lynch.
             p. cm. -- (Musical Instruments)
       Includes bibliographical references (p.) and index.
       ISBN 1-58810-234-3
       1. Keyboard instruments--Juvenile literature. [1. Keyboard instruments. 2. Piano] I. Title. II. Series.

ML549 .L96 2001
786'.19--dc21
                          2001000096

Acknowledgments
The publishers would like to thank the following for permission to reproduce photographs: Ace Photo Agency, p. 11; Corbis, p. 23; Gareth Boden, pp. 9, 28, 29; Lebrecht collection, pp. 20 (Dorothy Y Riess MD), 26 (Kate Mount); Photodisc, pp. 6, 7, 8, 18, 19; Photographer's Direct/ Bernard Epstein, p. 17; Redferns, pp. 5 (Patrick Ford), 14, 25 (Ebet Roberts), 27 (Patrick Ford); Rex Features, p. 4 (Nick Cunard); Robert Harding, pp. 10, 21; Stone, pp. 16 (Ian Shaw), 22; Superstock, p. 24; Trevor Clifford, p. 15.

Cover photograph reproduced with permission of Punchstock/ Brand X Pictures.

The publishers would like to thank Nancy Harris for her assistance in the preparation of this book.

Every effort has been made to contact copyright holders of any material reproduced in this book. Any omissions will be rectified in subsequent printings if notice is given to the publisher.

The paper used to print this book comes from sustainable sources.

Any words appearing in the text in bold, **like this**, are explained in the Glossary.

Contents

Making Music Together

There are many musical instruments in the world. Each instrument makes a different sound. We can make music together by playing these instruments in a band or an **orchestra**. An orchestra is a large group of musicians.

Bands and orchestras are made up of
different groups of instruments. One
of these groups is called keyboard
instruments. You may find them in
smaller bands such as this **jazz** band.

The piano and harpsichord are keyboard instruments. So are the organ and the **synthesizer**. A synthesizer is an electronic instrument. They are called keyboard instruments because they are all played using a keyboard.

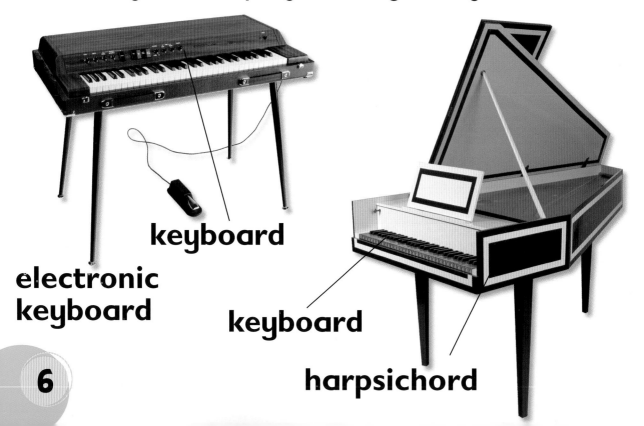

keyboard

electronic keyboard

keyboard

harpsichord

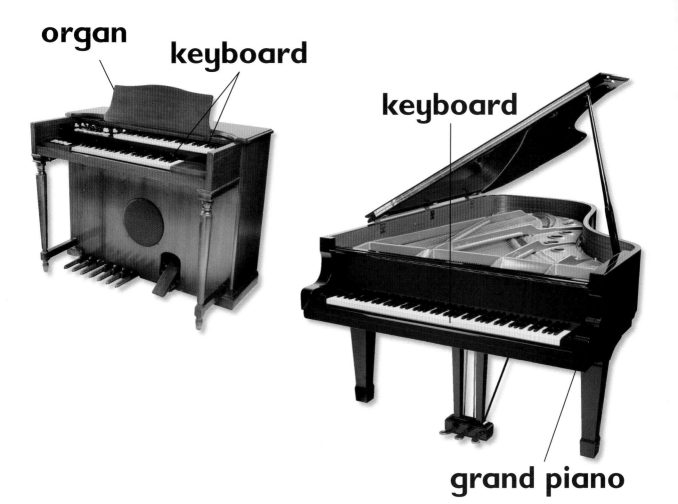

organ

keyboard

keyboard

grand piano

A keyboard has many keys. You
press the key to make a sound.
Each key makes a different sound.
This sound is a musical note.

The Piano

The piano is a popular keyboard instrument. Children often learn to play the piano with a music teacher.

You can play the piano with another person. This is called playing a duet. One player plays the keys on the left of the keyboard. The other plays the keys on the right.

Making a Noise

The piano has black keys and white keys. These keys are in a pattern. The keys on the left of the keyboard play lower notes. The keys on the right play higher notes.

Inside the piano there is a string for each key. When you press a key a hammer hits the string. The strings that play the lower notes are wider than the strings for the higher notes.

How the Sound Is Made

You push down a key. A hammer hits a string inside the piano. This makes the string move quickly from side to side.

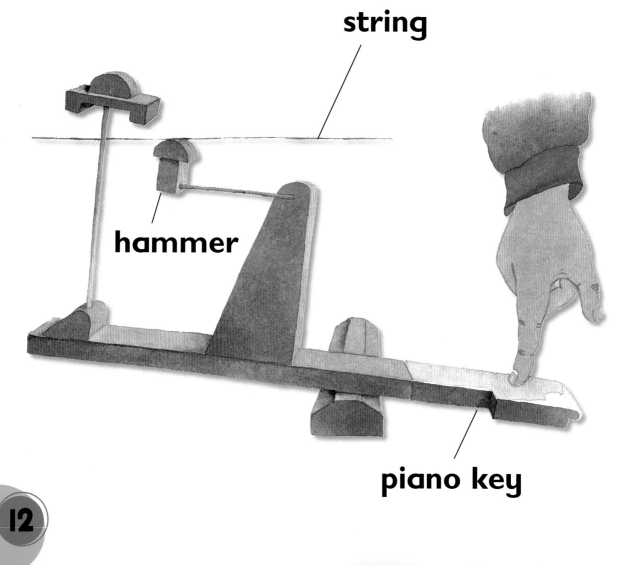

string

hammer

piano key

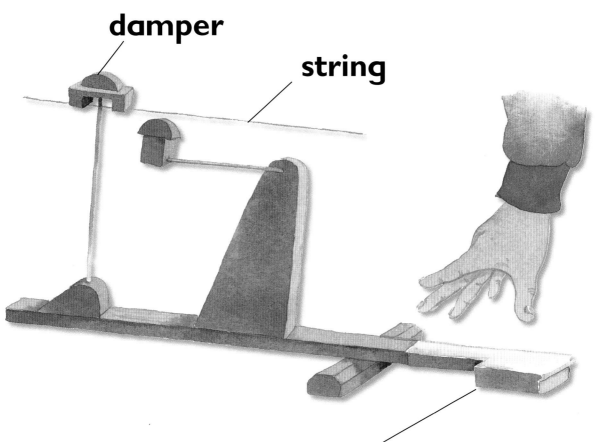

damper

string

piano key

The movement of the strings makes the air inside the piano **vibrate**. When air vibrates, it makes a sound. The sound stops when you lift your finger from the piano key. A piece of wood stops the string from vibrating. It is called a damper.

This is an **upright piano**. You can find upright pianos in many places. They are in schools, houses, and restaurants.

The grand piano is played in concerts. You can keep the lid of the grand piano open as you play. This makes the sound stronger and richer.

Piano Concert

In school, your teacher may play the piano to **accompany** (go with) singing. She may play it to accompany dancing or movement. She may play it for a **musical** you perform.

You may hear the piano on its own.
You may hear it with other musical
instruments. In a piano **trio** (three
musicians), you can hear the piano, the
violin, and the cello.

Types of Keyboards

The harpsichord has strings inside it. When you press a key, a small piece of wood inside the harpsichord **plucks** (pulls) the string.

The electric piano sounds very much like an **upright piano**. It does not make music using strings and hammers. The sound is made by an electronic **amplifier**.

Organs and Harmoniums

The organ has a keyboard. It is a keyboard instrument. It is also a wind instrument.

The harmonium is a kind of organ. It has **bellows** that hold the air. When you press the pedal you pump air into a **reed**. The reed **vibrates** and makes a sound.

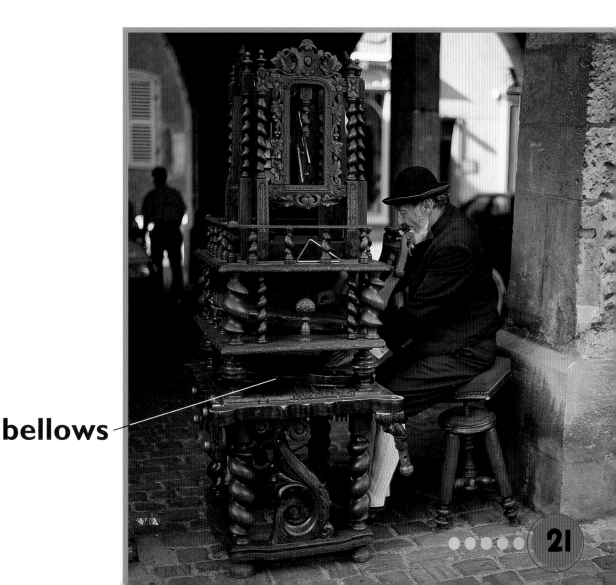

bellows

The Wider Family

To play the accordion you press the keyboard and buttons. At the same time, you push and pull the **bellows**. This makes the air move inside the accordion. This makes the sound.

The vibraphone has metal bars that look like a keyboard. You strike the bars using two hammers. You can hear the vibraphone in **jazz** music.

Famous Musicians and Composers

Mozart was a famous **composer**. A composer is a person who writes music. He started playing the harpsichord when he was four years old. He wrote a lot of music for the piano.

Stevie Wonder is a famous keyboard player. He is blind. He learned to play the piano when he was very young.

New Music

People play electronic keyboards in **jazz**, **rock**, and **pop** music today. Many keyboards have a drum **rhythm**. Keyboards can be linked to computers to play many new sounds.

Some musicians use **synthesizers** in rock and pop music. A synthesizer is an electronic instrument that can make many different sounds.

Sound Activity

- You can make up your own music on the piano.

- Make up some music that sounds like rain falling.

- Make it slow and gentle.

- Then make it faster and louder.

- Ask a grown-up to lift the lid of a piano.

- Then ask them to play some notes.

- Stand on a chair and look inside the piano.

- Can you see the hammers hit the strings?

Thinking About Keyboards

You can find the answers to all of these questions in this book.

1. Why are the instruments in this book called keyboard instruments?
2. What is a piano duet?
3. How do you play the accordion?
4. What is a harmonium?

More Books to Read

Knight, M. J. *Keyboards: Musical Instruments of the World.* Mankato, Minn: Smart Apple Media, 2005.

Pancella, Peggy. *Wolfgang Amadeus Mozart: Lives and Times.* Chicago: Heinemann Library, 2006.

Glossary

accompany to go with

amplifier something that changes electrical signals into sounds by sending them through a loudspeaker
You say *ampli-fire*

bellows pump used to direct air into the soundpipes of an instrument

composer person who writes music

jazz old style of music from the United States that is often made up as it is played

musical play set to music, with songs and dancing

orchestra large group of musicians who play their musical instruments together
You say *ork-es-tra*

plucks pulls

pop music music of the last 50 years. A lot of people like this music.

reed thin strip of cane or metal

rhythm repeated beats or sounds that make a pattern
You say *rith-um*

rock music type of pop music with a strong beat

synthesizer electronic instrument that can make or change many different sounds
You say *sintha-size-er*

trio music for three players or a group of three musicians
You say *tree-o*

upright piano piano in which the strings stand up against the soundboard

vibrate move up and down or from side to side very quickly

Index

A
accordion 22
amplifier 19

B
bands 4, 5
bellows 21, 22

C
cello 17
composers 24

D
damper 13
duet 9

E
electric piano 19
electronic keyboard
26

G
grand piano 15

H
hammers 11, 12, 23,
29

harmonium 21
harpsichord 6, 18

J
jazz 5, 23, 26

K
keyboard 6, 7, 22,
23, 26
keys 7, 10, 11, 13,
18

M
Mozart, Wolfgang
Amadeus 24

O
orchestras 4, 5
organ 6, 7, 20

P
piano 6, 8–17, 19,
24, 25, 28–9
pop music 26, 27

R
reed 21

rhythm 26
rock music 26, 27

S
strings 11, 12, 13,
18, 19, 29
synthesizer 6, 27

T
trio 17

U
upright piano 14, 19

V
vibraphone 23
vibration 13, 21
violin 17

W
wind instrument 20
Wonder, Stevie 25